AF291358

BIG PICTURE PRESS

First published in the UK in 2026 by Big Picture Press,
an imprint of Bonnier Books UK
5th Floor, HYLO, 105 Bunhill Row,
London, EC1Y 8LZ
The authorised representative in the EEA
is Bonnier Books UK (Ireland) Limited.
Registered office address:
Block B, The Crescent Building
Northwood, Santry
Dublin 9, D09 C6X8, Ireland
compliance@bonnierbooks.ie
www.bonnierbooks.co.uk

Originally published under the title
La Terre racontée aux enfants © Gallimard Jeunesse, 2024
Text copyright © 2024 by Pierrick Graviou & Érik Orsenna
Illustration copyright © 2024 by Stéphane Kiehl
Design copyright © 2026 by Big Picture Press

1 3 5 7 9 10 8 6 4 2

ISBN 978-1-83587-450-9

This book was typeset in Centra No.2
The illustrations were painted digitally

Translated by Russell McLean
Consulted by Dougal Dixon
Edited by Charlie Wilson
Designed by Sarah Crookes
Production by Ché Creasey

Printed in China

ONCE UPON A PLANET

Pierrick Graviou & Érik Orsenna

Illustrated by Stéphane Kiehl

B P P

Once upon a time, there was a planet
– a shimmering blue world spinning in space.
This planet was called Earth.

The story of Earth is the most incredible tale of all.
It's the story of vast oceans and rolling seas, towering
mountains and shimmering lakes, ancient glaciers and
winding rivers, sun-baked deserts and deep forests.

It's the story of sea creatures gliding through
ancient waters, of trees reaching skyward and flowers
bursting into bloom. It's the story of insects buzzing,
reptiles basking, birds soaring and beasts roaming –
from the shaggy mammoth to the mighty ape.

It is the story of the blue planet.
Blue, like the oceans that blanket most of its surface.
Perhaps the most beautiful planet in the Universe.
And yet, Earth's story began with chaos,
13.8 billion years ago...

Long ago, a mighty explosion – the Big Bang –
gave birth to the Universe. In the beginning, everything
was a thick and boiling soup of light and matter, swelling,
stretching, growing. As it cooled, the haze began to clear.
Within the mist, clumps and clouds formed – and in those
quiet pockets of space, the first stars were born.

These stars were mighty forges, crafting atoms
– tiny grains that fit together like building blocks.
Atoms are everywhere: in the water we drink, the air
we breathe, the rocks beneath our feet, even in the
pages of this book. They are in every plant and
every animal. All born from stardust.

Among all the stars in the Universe,
one burned bright for 4.5 billion years –
a golden orb that warmed a small blue world.
This star, shining even in daylight, was the Sun.

Around it danced eight planets. Jupiter, Saturn,
Uranus and Neptune – great swirling worlds
of gas and ice. Mercury, Venus, Earth and Mars –
rocky planets, closest to the fire.

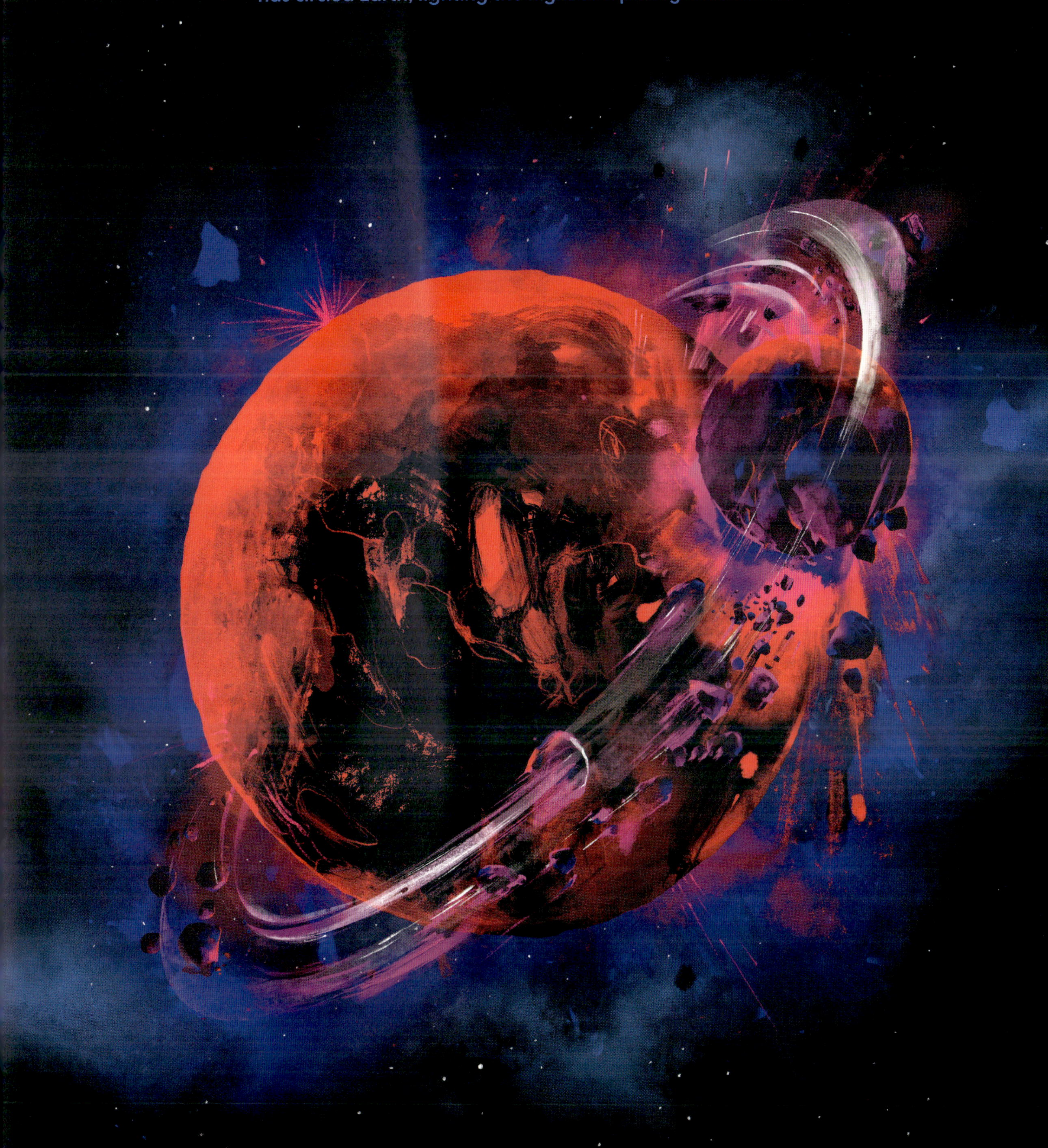

But one day, disaster struck. Earth collided with a
wandering planet we now call Theia. The impact was so fierce,
it shattered both worlds. Fragments of rock flew into space,
spinning and swirling through the void. Slowly, they gathered
into a glowing sphere – the Moon. And ever since, the Moon
has circled Earth, lighting the night and pulling at the tides.

Bombarded by countless meteorites, Earth melted into a blazing ocean of rock. The surface boiled and bubbled, glowing red with heat. Slowly, lava cooled and hardened, forming a fragile crust. But deep below, rivers of lava surged, reshaping the young planet from within.

volcanoes spewed lava and ash, filling the sky with
choking clouds of gas and great geysers of steam.
And then – the rain began. Rain without end, falling for
days, months, years. The water swallowed the land,
rising higher and higher, until it formed the very first
ocean. No islands or continents. No algae, shells or fish.
Just a silent, lonely sea beneath a stormy sky.

Time passed. The volcanoes rumbled and rose,
pushing higher and higher until they broke
through the ocean's surface. The first islands
were born – few at first, then many, scattered
like stepping stones across the sea.

With each eruption, the islands grew and gathered,
slowly joining together. And so, the continents began to take
shape, rising from the deep to form the face of the Earth.

Out of the chaos, life appeared. No one knows exactly when, how or where – it remains one of the Universe's great mysteries. Some believe it began with complex molecules that could reproduce, absorbing raw materials from the water. These evolved into tiny single-celled beings, including bacteria, invisible to the eye yet countless. Living in colonies, they quietly shaped the future of life on Earth.

Even as life evolved, the Earth remained without oxygen.
Then, remarkable single-celled beings harnessed sunlight
and learned to breathe in a new way – absorbing carbon
dioxide and releasing oxygen into the water and air.
Invisible but vital, this gas would eventually fill the
skies and make life as we know it possible.

Around 2.4 billion years ago, the planet froze.
Ice spread across the globe, thickening with
time, until the continents lay buried beneath
an icy shell several kilometres deep.

The world was locked in silence,
wrapped in white. A frozen Earth,
waiting for the warmth to return.

The bacteria – Earth's only inhabitants – slowed their work and waited for better days. But the volcanoes did not rest. Their fires still burned beneath the ice, rumbling in the deep. Little by little, their heat melted the frozen Earth, warming the world once more. And life, patient and persistent, began to stir again.

After surviving the great freeze, the bacteria awoke.
Countless colonies stirred in the warming seas,
and something remarkable began to happen.
Some joined together, forming new kinds of cells
– and life stirred beneath the waves.

Inside these tiny cells was a nucleus – a little heart of life. The cells joined together, forming larger living beings. Fossils of these creatures, nearly 600 million years old, have been found – perhaps worms, sponges or jellyfish drifting through the seas of long ago.

All the animals that lived then were creatures of
the sea. They drifted with the currents, their bodies
soft and fragile. But around 540 million years ago,
new forms of life appeared. Some hid inside shells;
others grew hard armour on their backs.

Among these ancient lifeforms were trilobites –
creatures like giant woodlice, crawling across the
ocean floor. With eyes that searched for food and
armour that shimmered like polished stone, they
wandered the deep. When danger came, they curled
into tight balls, safe inside their shining shells.

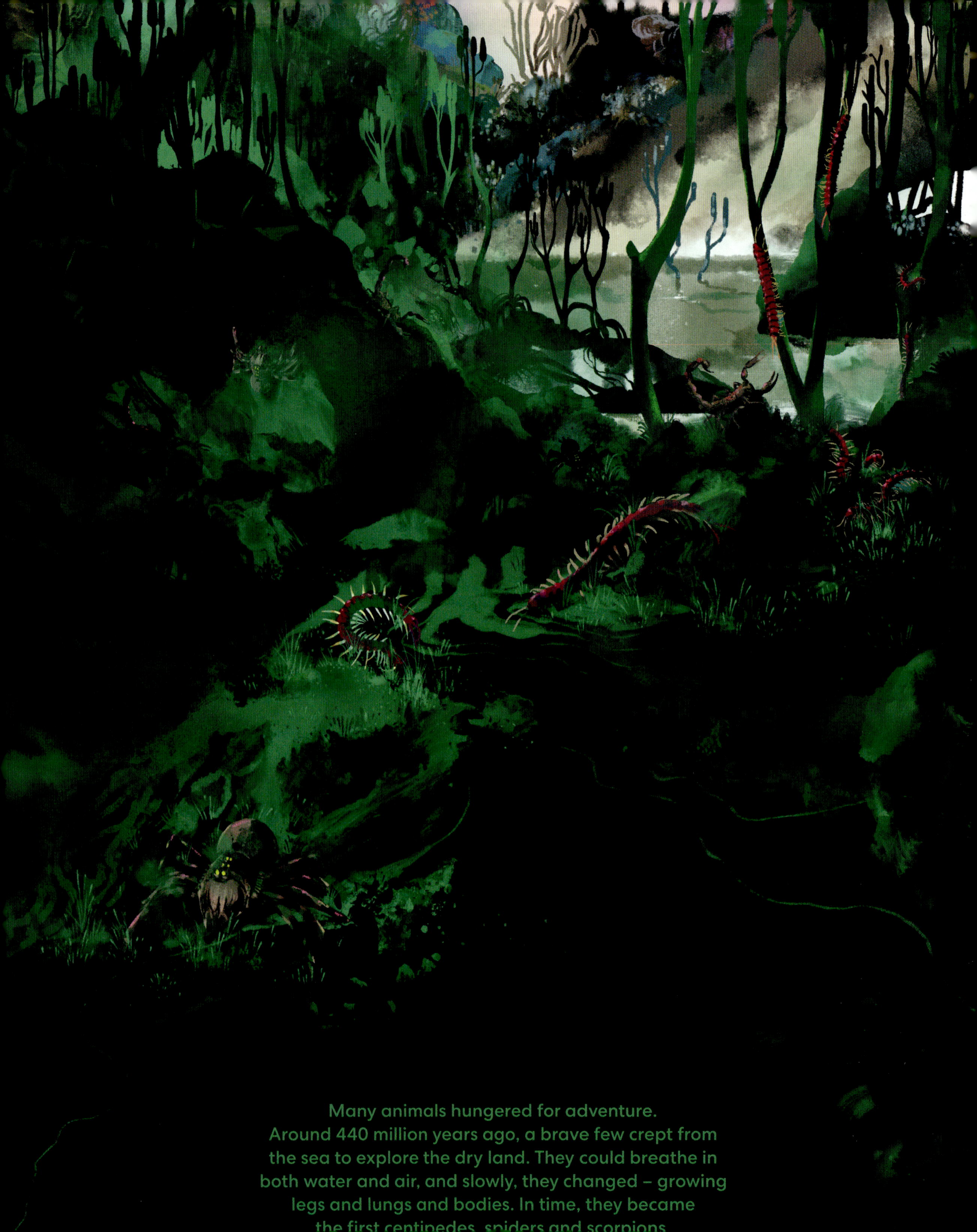
Many animals hungered for adventure.
Around 440 million years ago, a brave few crept from
the sea to explore the dry land. They could breathe in
both water and air, and slowly, they changed – growing
legs and lungs and bodies. In time, they became
the first centipedes, spiders and scorpions.

But these tiny adventurers were not the first
living things to begin their journey upon the land.
Long before them, lichens, mosses and fungi had
already made their home there. For thirty million years,
they spread across the rocky surface. Slowly, our blue
planet grew greener... becoming ever more alive.

Battling against great swirling forces deep within
the Earth, mighty continents crept towards each
other on a slow, silent journey. They moved no faster
than fingernails grow – inch by inch, year by year.

And then, 350 million years ago, they met in a
thunderous crash, and the world was forever changed.

The force of the crush was colossal. Rocks cracked
and crumpled, rising into mountains as tall as the Alps.
An ancient range rose between the colliding continents
of Europe and North America. Though worn down by time,
you can still see its traces in Brittany's rugged coast and
the mountains of Scotland and Norway.

Three hundred million years ago, Europe lay near
the Equator. In the valleys between snowy peaks,
heat shimmered, and rain fell gently. Below, in the
swampy forests, trees soared skyward – so tall that
sunlight barely touched the ground. It was a world
of shadows and giants, lush and humming with life.

Beneath towering trees, strange creatures crept
through the undergrowth – amphibians that lived in
water but breathed air. They hunted giant insects:
centipedes as long as grown men and dragonflies
with wings as wide as a child's arms.

In a never-ending dance, the continents drifted across
Earth's face. Sometimes they drew apart as the ocean
rose up between them; sometimes they drew close,
raising mountains where they met.

Then, about 250 million years ago, they gathered
together, forming one vast supercontinent: Pangaea.
A world united, just for a moment in time.

During this period, Earth blazed like a furnace. Pangaea stretched dry and bare – a vast desert of dust and stone. But along the ocean's edge, the air grew softer, moister, and forests flourished thick and green. There, in the shade of ancient trees, the first dinosaurs appeared – and the first mammals followed – before roaming across the endless land.

Around 200 million years ago, the continents began to drift apart. Oceans formed, volcanoes erupted and the climate changed. Many species vanished – but dinosaurs adapted and thrived. They roamed every continent, from cool poles to warm lowlands, mountains to coastal shores.

This was the true age of dinosaurs. *Brachiosaurus* stretched its long neck to reach the highest leaves. *Stegosaurus* grew bony frills and a spiked tail for defence. In the skies, pterosaurs soared – flying reptiles that fed on insects and seized small, unwary mammals that ventured from their shelters.

Amongst the great predators, small mammals –
no larger than rats or squirrels – emerged into the light.
Still fearing the thunderous footsteps that shook the earth,
they hid in burrows and forest shadows. Above them,
feathered creatures with clawed wings – dinosaur-like birds
such as *Archaeopteryx* – fluttered between branches,
their calls echoing through the stillness.

These tiny mammals and primitive birds were bold.
Soon it would be their turn to roam the land and fill
the skies with sound. Just as dinosaurs once ruled
the Earth, mammals would one day reign.

Beneath the waves, ichthyosaurs cut
through the water, hunting fish and
armoured ammonites – marine creatures
protected by hard, coiled shells.

In the ocean depths, tiny organisms lived among
microscopic algae. Swept together by swirling
currents, they formed plankton – a drifting feast
for darting fish and curly-shelled ammonites.
Even mighty sea reptiles like plesiosaurs joined
the banquet, gulping seawater rich with life.

Volcanoes raged, belching ash and smoke that darkened
the skies and hid the Sun behind a curtain of grey.
The world grew cold. Whether scaled or feathered,
the dinosaurs had little shelter from the freeze.
And slowly, silently, they began to die out.

Then, disaster struck. Sixty-six million years ago,
a giant meteorite tore through the sky and crashed
into Earth – into what is now present-day Mexico.
The impact shook the planet. Fires raged, burning
the forests, and ash buried the plants. Plant-eating
dinosaurs starved, and the meat-eaters soon followed.
Only birds – feathered dinosaurs – found ways to
survive. Nearly all other dinosaurs, and many other
creatures, vanished from the Earth.

After the meteor struck and the age of dinosaurs ended,
Earth changed slowly over millions of years. In East Africa,
forests began to thin. Trees gave way to open grasslands
beneath a wide, golden sky. As the landscape shifted,
some primates left the safety of the trees. They walked
on two feet, upright and curious, scanning the horizon.
These were the australopithecines: small, clever mammals
beginning a new journey across the land.

Along the shimmering shores of ancient East African lakes, the australopithecines made their home. Less than three million years ago, they gave rise to the first humans. At first, these early people fed only on plants, but soon learned to hunt – tracking prey across grasslands, forests and mountains. Step by step, they left Africa behind, exploring new lands and spreading across the globe. A journey had begun – one that would shape the future of the Earth.

Twenty thousand years ago, a deep cold gripped the
Earth. Icy winds swept across the land, reaching even
the warm shores of the Mediterranean. Mammoths and
woolly rhinoceroses trudged through the frost, wrapped
in thick fur and layers of fat. But not all creatures were
so well protected. To survive, humans adapted – wearing
the hides of animals, stitching warmth from the wild.

Glaciers stretched across vast parts of Europe and
North America, reshaping the land with their icy grip.
Sea levels fell by over a hundred metres, and the Channel
lay bare – a wide, frozen path between continents. For a time,
it was possible to walk from mainland Europe to England
across the cold, dry seabed. But this did not last. The ice
melted, the seas rose and the world changed once more.

Over time, the mighty glaciers retreated.
Oceans rose, swallowing coastlines and reshaping
the land. The Americas drifted farther from Europe and
Africa as the Atlantic Ocean widened, centimetre by
centimetre. Mountain chains like the Alps, the Pyrenees
and the Himalayas continued to grow. Earth's surface
never stopped changing. Life evolved – some species
vanished, others arrived to take their place.

But today, something different is happening.
Strange animals are disrupting our planet's natural
rhythms. These animals – you know them well – are us.
Humans have changed the planet: cutting forests,
polluting air and sea and warming the Earth
faster than ever before.

Yet we can also care for it, if we learn to live in
harmony with every living thing. We must act quickly,
if we wish to keep living on this beautiful world.
Change is still possible.